How to Reach Your Favorite Star

▼▼▼▼▼

by
Fiona Fox

Checkerboard Press
• • • • • • •
New York

How <u>Do</u> You Reach Your Favorite Star?

*N*othing is more fun than connecting with somebody you care about! And if it's a celebrity, it's a special thrill to receive an answer to a letter or postcard. But getting in touch with celebrities isn't always the easiest business! This book will help your search. Here are a few pointers:

➤ It's always a good idea to send a self-addressed, stamped envelope (SASE) if you want a reply. Along with your letter, simply enclose a stamped envelope addressed to yourself. If you're writing from overseas or Canada, you'll need international postage coupons instead, which you can buy at any post office. The SASE should give you a quicker reply than if you don't include one, and in some cases it's necessary to get any reply at all!

➤ Not all celebrities have fan clubs, but when you send a letter to your favorite star, you can ask for any fan club information available.

➤ Keep in mind that, just like all of us, stars sometimes move, alter their business addresses, or change their fan club directors and addresses. Usually, though, the postal service will forward mail that has been sent to an old address to the star's new address.

➤ Remember, stars are always glad to hear from you since it's your support that has helped put them where they are today!

So don't be shy! Use the resources in this book to find out about your faves, then get down to it and send off a letter to all of them! You just might be surprised by the return mail you get!

Copyright © 1992 by RGA Publishing Group, Inc. All rights reserved.
ISBN: 1-56288-330-5

Library of Congress Catalog Card Number: 92-17291

Printed in the United States of America   10 9 8 7 6 5 4 3 2 1

Published by Checkerboard Press, Inc.
30 Vesey Street, New York, NY 10007

Contents

▼▼▼▼▼▼▼▼▼▼▼▼▼▼▼▼▼▼▼▼▼▼▼

Paula Abdul

So You Want to Know —

What Paula does on a weekend? When she's in town, she goes roller-skating on the Venice Beach boardwalk.

Super Stats

➤ Birth date: June 19, 1963
➤ Born and raised in: Los Angeles
➤ Family: mom, Lorraine; sister, Wendy
➤ Height: 5'2"
➤ Loves: singing, dancing, exercising, and touring
➤ Fave foods: fruit and mixed berry yogurt

*A*fter graduating from high school, Paula made the Laker Girls, the Los Angeles Lakers' basketball cheerleading squad. She was soon choreographing the dynamite moves of that flashy group. The Jacksons (especially Michael and Janet) noticed her hot moves out on the court at halftime. And before she knew it, her talent at choreographing music videos for the Jacksons led Paula to her own record contract and a sizzling career in show biz!

Cool Tunes

➤ **Albums:** *Forever Your Girl, Shut Up and Dance, Spellbound*

Notable Quote

"I'm very committed to my career, but I'm looking forward to the day when I can have a family."

Paula Abdul
P.O. Box 420755
San Francisco, CA
94142

Or try:
Paula Abdul Fan Club
14755 Ventura Blvd. #1-710
Sherman Oaks, CA 91403

Bryan Adams

Super Stats

➤ Full name: Bryan Guy Adams
➤ Birth date: November 5, 1959
➤ Native of: Vancouver, British Columbia (Canada)
➤ Outstanding achievements: first Canadian artist ever to top the U.S., Canadian, and British charts simultaneously; his single "(Everything I Do) I Do It For You" has sold more than 10 million copies worldwide

Cool Tunes

➤ **Albums:** *Bryan Adams, Cuts Like a Knife, You Want It, Reckless, Into the Fire, Waking Up the Neighbours*

So You Want to Know —

The facts behind Bryan's hit "(Everything I Do) I Do It For You"? The song was actually composed for the movie *Robin Hood: Prince of Thieves* by music man Michael Kamen, who contacted Bryan to write lyrics for it. The hit was so hot that it soared to #1 on the U.S. charts in five weeks!

Notable Quote

"My songs are part of my imagination....I'm sorry that they weren't translated better to other people, but they were satisfying to me."

Here's a guy who's been cranking out hits for years! And it looks as though Bryan definitely can't stop this hot rock thing he's started! He's been going strong since the age of 15, when he worked as front man for the band Sweeney Todd. He first made it big on his own with a little disco dance tune called, not surprisingly, "Let Me Take You Dancin' " —and that was way back in 1979!

Bryan Adams
Adams News
406-68 Water St.
Vancouver, B.C.
Canada V6B 1A4

Andre Agassi

Super Stats

➤ Birth date: April 29, 1970
➤ Born and raised in: Las Vegas, Nevada
➤ Current residence: Las Vegas and Bradenton, Florida, at the Nick Bollettieri Tennis Academy
➤ Hair/eye color: brown-streaked blond/brown
➤ Height: 5'11"
➤ Family: father, Emmanuel ("Mike"), is a former Las Vegas show master and Iranian Olympic boxer; mother, Elizabeth, works for the state of Nevada; sister, Tamee, plays collegiate tennis; brother, Philip, travels with Andre as his personal manager
➤ Turned pro: May 1, 1986
➤ Earliest achievement: At two years old, he could serve in a full court!

➤ Highest doubles ranking: 215
➤ Fan mail: receives 1,500 to 2,000 letters a week
➤ Active supporter of: Fellowship of Christian Athletes
➤ Transportation: Cars and motorcycles are Andre's passion. He's got at least nine different vehicles, including a Harley-Davidson and a $400,000 black Vector with bat-wing doors, a 12-speaker stereo system, a TV monitor, and a rearview camera!

So You Want to Know —

About Andre's court capers? He's got a flair for the dramatic—blowing kisses to the crowd and throwing his acid-washed Nike shorts to fans in the stands while tossing back his long locks of blond hair.

*K*nown for his aggressive topspin forehand, tennis ace Andre Agassi gave the game a shot of adrenaline when he appeared on the scene! At only 18, he wowed the world by winning six major tournaments, reaching the semifinals in both the French and U.S. Opens, and shooting from number 91 to become the number 3 player in the world. At 22 years old, he became the 1992 Wimbledon champion in men's singles. Although he's got his share of critics, Andre's flamboyant style has made him a household name as well as a major heartthrob!

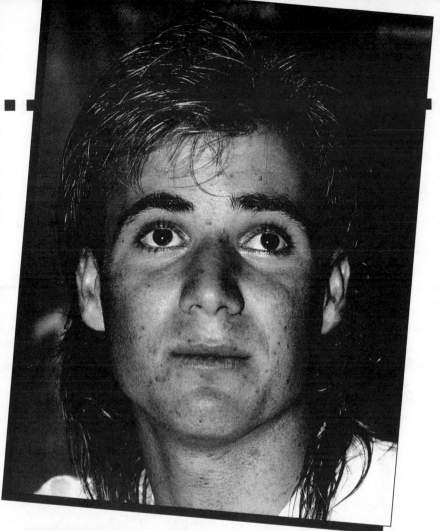

Notable Quote

"I'm blessed with a talent, and I have an obligation to the Lord to make the most of it."

● ●

Andre Agassi
c/o International
Management Group
One Erieview Plaza
Suite 1300
Cleveland, OH 44114-1782

Andre's Court Club
P.O. Box 4297
Portland, OR 97208-4298

Send a self-addressed, stamped envelope and request club information.

7

● ●

Sean Astin

➤ Full name: Sean Patrick Astin
➤ Birth date: February 25, 1971
➤ Birthplace: Santa Monica, California
➤ Raised in: Los Angeles area
➤ Family: dad, John Astin, is a writer, director, and actor (he starred as Gomez in "The Addams Family" TV series); mom is actress Patty Duke; younger brother, Mackenzie; five stepbrothers and stepsisters
➤ Fave pastimes: baseball, waterskiing, snow skiing, working on his computer

Notable Quote

"Acting is a lot of fun, but when you work with a lot of kids your own age it's a lot more competitive… but sometimes that inspires you to do better work."

Cool Credits

➤ **TV:** *ABC Afterschool Special* "Please Don't Hit Me, Mom," the miniseries "Rules of Marriage"
➤ **Film highlights**: *Goonies, The War of the Roses, Memphis Belle, Toy Soldiers, Encino Man, Where the Day Takes You*

Having two parents in show biz, Sean has been exposed to acting since he was born. So it's not surprising he would go for it himself. His first professional experience was in an *ABC Afterschool Special* when he was only seven. His boyish energy, natural charm, and obvious talent have kept him super-busy in "the biz" ever since!

So You Want to Know —

Sean's little-known credits? In the fourth grade he acted in *Annie Get Your Gun* and two years later played Snoopy in *You're a Good Man, Charlie Brown.*

Sean Astin
c/o CAA
9830 Wilshire Blvd.
Beverly Hills, CA 90212

Sebastian Bach

As lead vocalist in Skid Row (one of hard rock's hottest bands), Sebastian—or "Bas," as he's known to his friends—is a golden angel. His voice is one good reason this guy has made it to the top, but another is his sheer determination. When he shines onstage, he's unforgettable!

Notable Quote

"For most people, rock shows are an escape from reality, but when you do it every night, your reality is mayhem!"

So You Want to Know —

What the other band members of Skid Row often call their wild lead singer? Because of his outrageously loud-mouthed stage antics, Bas is frequently referred to as "Marshall Mouth"!

Super Stats

➤ Real name: Sebastian Bierk
➤ Birth date: April 3, 1968
➤ Birthplace: Freeport, the Bahamas
➤ Height: 6'3"
➤ Family: younger brother, Zack, lives in Ontario; younger sister, Dylan, is a model in Europe; also has a son, Paris, with his girlfriend, Maria
➤ Fave musicians: Hanoi Rocks, Mötley Crüe, Janis Joplin
➤ Earlier rock bands he belonged to: VO5 and Kid Wicked
➤ Fave breakfast food: chili
➤ Transportation: a black Camaro

Cool Tunes

➤ **Albums:** *Skid Row* (over 3 million copies sold), *Slave to the Grind*

Sebastian Bach
c/o Skid Row
Atlantic Records
9229 Sunset Blvd. #900
Los Angeles, CA 90069

Boris Becker

Super Stats

➤ Birth date: November 22, 1967
➤ Birthplace: Leiman, Germany
➤ Current residences: Monte Carlo and Leiman
➤ Height: 6'3"
➤ Family: father, Karl-Heinz, is an avid amateur tennis player and an architect; mother, Elvira
➤ Age when he began tennis training: three years old
➤ Other interests: soccer, reading, going to the movies, listening to rock music
➤ Dislikes: when fans gang up on him
➤ Cool career coups: in 1985, at 18 years old, he became youngest person ever to win the Wimbledon Grand Slam event; he also won at Wimbledon in 1986 and 1989

Big, blond, and determined to win, tennis star Boris is a national hero in his homeland. He's got a scorching serve and is known as a real power player. Where once he seemed to come on like a big, affectionate puppy, he has grown up and refined his style. Now he gets noticed for his incredible abilities on the court, his composure under pressure, and his occasionally awesome acrobatics.

Notable Quote

"It's very difficult to be German sometimes. Because of their guilt, the Germans feel they have to do something special. I have to behave better than my opponents."

So You Want to Know —

How Boris describes his schedule? "Practicing, eating, sleeping, and practicing."

Boris Becker
c/o TV Enterprises
251 E. 49th St.
New York, NY 10017

Mayim Bialik

Super Stats

➤ Birth date: December 12, 1975
➤ Birthplace: San Diego, California
➤ Raised in: Los Angeles
➤ Family: parents, Beverly and Barry; older brother, Isaac
➤ Interests: video and arcade games, shopping, listening to music, dancing
➤ Musical instruments: plays trumpet and piano
➤ Fave singer: George Michael
➤ Early ambition: to be a newscaster

So You Want to Know —

Mayim's little-known credits? She has provided the voices for Edgar the Hedgehog in Hanna-Barbera's cartoon pilot "Dapplewood Odyssey" and for "Peanuts" cartoon character Peppermint Patty on a national commercial.

Notable Quote

"I think it's important for people to know that even a kid can make a difference. If more people would read the newspaper and pay attention to the news on a daily basis, I think they couldn't help but get involved...."

Cool Credits

➤ **TV:** title roles in "Molloy" and "Blossom," co-starring roles in "Beauty and the Beast," "Facts of Life," "Webster," "Once a Hero," "MacGyver"
➤ **Film:** *Beaches, Pumpkin Head, Halmani*

*T*alk about talent! Besides being a dancer, singer, actor, musician, and mime, this girl's got the super smarts, too! Mayim's active in many worthwhile causes, including animal rights and care for the homeless, and she's a U.S. representative for the United Nations International School's program for better relations among people of all nations.

Mayim Bialik
c/o Burton Entertainment
1419 Peerless Pl. #120
Los Angeles, CA 90035

Garth Brooks

Super Stats

➤ Full name: Troyal Garth Brooks
➤ Birth date: February 7, 1962
➤ Raised in: Yukon, Oklahoma
➤ Family: dad, Troyal, is a petroleum engineer/draftsman; mom, Colleen, was once a country singer; five older siblings; married Sandy Mahr in 1987
➤ Education: attended Oklahoma State University on a track scholarship
➤ Fashion style: pressed Wrangler jeans and 10-gallon Stetson hats
➤ Fave possession: his collection of John Wayne movie videos
➤ Music idols: George Strait, George Jones, Billy Joel, James Taylor, Dan Fogelberg

J ust a good ol' country boy, Garth traveled to Nashville in 1987, where he got a last-minute singing gig at a benefit performance. A Capitol Records executive was in the audience, and the next thing Garth knew, he had a recording contract!

Cool Tunes

➤ **Albums:** *Christmas Standards, Vols. 1 & 2; Family Christmas Treasury; Garth Brooks; No Fences; Ropin' the Wind*

Notable Quote

"People see me as a real person, as the guy next door, and as evidence that the American dream is very much alive...."

So You Want to Know —

Where Garth is living these days? He and his wife, Sandy, recently moved into a 6,700-square-foot home on 20 acres of land on the outskirts of Nashville.

Garth Brooks
P.O. Box 507
Goodlettsville, TN 37070

Chris Burke

■ ■ ■ ■ ■ ■ ■ ■ ■ ■ ■ ■ ■ ■ ■ ■ ■ ■ ■

*S*tarring in a popular TV drama is something nobody would have expected of Chris. When he was born with the genetic deficiency, Down's syndrome, his doctor believed he should be institutionalized. But Chris's family refused to consider such an option. A good thing, too! Now, Chris is well-known for his role as Corky on "Life Goes On." He's a true inspiration!

So You Want to Know —

How Chris got his part on "Life Goes On"? Chris was inspired by a Down's syndrome boy he saw acting on TV and wrote to him. He and the boy, Jason Kingsley, began a correspondence and finally met. Jason's mother, who worked in TV, recommended Chris for a telefilm called "Desperate." Chris won the role, and later the "Life Goes On" series was created especially for him.

Super Stats

➤ Birth date: August 26
➤ Born and raised in: New York City
➤ Current residence: Los Angeles
➤ Family: dad, Frank, a retired New York Police Department inspector; mom, Marian; two sisters and one brother
➤ Other activities: a volunteer at a camp for the handicapped, a spokesman for the National Down's Syndrome Congress and for the National Down's Syndrome Society

Notable Quote

"I have a slight case of Down's syndrome. I call it 'Up syndrome.'"

Chris Burke
c/o "Life Goes On"
Capital Cities/ABC, Inc.
2040 Avenue of the Stars
Century City, CA 90067

Naomi Campbell

*B*eautiful Brit Naomi has become one of the most in-demand models doing the international beat. Discovered when she was 14, Naomi had made the pages of the British *Elle* by 15. Today, she shuttles from one fashion capital to the next, making at least $15,000 for a stroll down a runway in Paris, Milan, or New York.

Notable Quote

"If you're not dedicated, it shows in your face and the picture. You can see every little thought."

Super Stats

➤ Birth date: May 22, 1970
➤ Born and raised in: London, England
➤ Height: 5'9"
➤ Family: Her mother, formerly a ballet dancer, was born in Jamaica and moved to England before Naomi was born. Naomi knows very little about her father, who left before she was born.
➤ Education: studied at the London Academy of Performing Arts
➤ Romantic adventures: She had a brief relationship with former heavyweight boxing champ Mike Tyson. She now sees actor Robert DeNiro as regularly as her jet-setting schedule will allow!
➤ Most exotic location: Lanzarote, on top of a volcano in Spain
➤ Fave cover: French *Vogue*, August 1989, because she was the first ethnic model ever to appear there

So You Want to Know —

Naomi's net worth in dollars and cents? Although she says, "I never discuss figures," experts estimate she makes more than $1.7 million per year.

Naomi Campbell
c/o Elite Model Management Corp.
111 E. 22nd St.
New York, NY 10010

Jennifer Capriati

▼▼▼▼▼▼▼▼▼▼▼▼▼

*E*ven the old masters get a little nervous when Jennifer lets go with her serve—it's been clocked at 95 miles per hour! Her dad introduced her to the game when she was three, and by the time she was five, she was working out daily with a ball machine and being coached by Jimmy Evert, Chris Evert's dad. Jennifer works hard at having fun on the tennis court—she's got the juice!

Notable Quote

"I have no fear."

So You Want to Know —

What a typical day for Jennifer Capriati is like? She goes to school for five hours, then has three hours of tennis practice and one hour of Nautilus workout. After that she might hit the video store to chill out with a movie.

Super Stats

➤ Birth date: March 29, 1976
➤ Birthplace: Long Island, New York
➤ Family: father, Stefano, is a real estate developer and her manager; mother, Denise, is a flight attendant; younger brother, Steven
➤ Fave movies: *Big, Ghost,* and *Pretty Woman*
➤ Fave jewelry: a gold bracelet that's inscribed "Love, Chris," which was given to her by former tennis champ Chris Evert
➤ Turned pro: March 5, 1990

Career Coups

➤ At 14, became youngest ever to be ranked in top ten
➤ In 1991, at 15, became youngest-ever female semifinalist at Wimbledon

Jennifer Capriati
c/o International Management Group
One Erieview Plaza
Suite 1300
Cleveland, OH 44114-1782

Mariah Carey

Notable Quote

"If you don't believe in yourself, you never get anywhere. That's one thing my mother taught me."

So You Want to Know —

Mariah's track record on her first album out? Her 1990 debut LP, *Mariah Carey*, sold more than 6 million copies, had four #1 hit singles, and earned Mariah Grammys as Best New Artist and Best Pop Female Vocalist!

Super Stats

➤ Birth date: March 27, 1970
➤ Birthplace: New York City
➤ Family: her mom, Patricia, a former mezzo-soprano with the New York City Opera, raised Mariah alone
➤ Personality: so shy it's hard for her even to get up on a stage and perform!
➤ Other jobs she's had: worked as a hostess, hat-check girl, and waitress
➤ Outstanding achievement: received two Grammys for her first LP
➤ Musical influences: Gladys Knight, Aretha Franklin, Minnie Riperton, Edwina Hawkins, Stevie Wonder, her mom

Cool Tunes

➤ **Albums:** *Mariah Carey, Emotions*

By the age of four, little Mariah was completely clear about what her future held: success as a super songstress. She followed her dream diligently, and her mom gave her the courage she needed to believe in herself and go for it. The day after Mariah graduated from high school, she moved to Manhattan and embarked on the magical musical tour that has taken her to the very top!

Mariah Carey
Columbia Records
P. O. Box 4450
New York, NY 10101-4450

Gabrielle Carteris

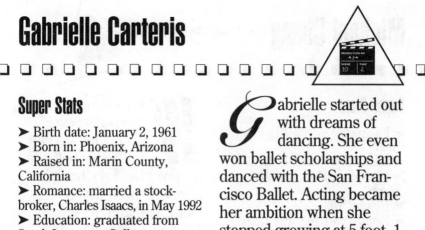

Super Stats

➤ Birth date: January 2, 1961
➤ Born in: Phoenix, Arizona
➤ Raised in: Marin County, California
➤ Romance: married a stockbroker, Charles Isaacs, in May 1992
➤ Education: graduated from Sarah Lawrence College
➤ Causes she's involved with: AIDS, Mothers Against Drunk Driving
➤ Fave actors: Meryl Streep, Spencer Tracy, Katharine Hepburn
➤ Transportation: a silver Honda Accord

Cool Credits

➤ **TV:** three *ABC Afterschool Specials*, "Another World," "Beverly Hills, 90210"

So You Want to Know —

What other kinds of interesting things Gabrielle is into? She's a major mime whiz! When she was 16, she traveled all over Europe as part of a mime troupe.

*G*abrielle started out with dreams of dancing. She even won ballet scholarships and danced with the San Francisco Ballet. Acting became her ambition when she stopped growing at 5 foot, 1 inch, and was considered too short to be a professional dancer. Now she has the kind of fame that'd make anybody feel like dancing!

Notable Quote

"I personally really believe in an education. We have to learn to be aware and involved with the world."

Gabrielle Carteris
"Beverly Hills, 90210"
P.O. Box 5600
Beverly Hills, CA 90209

Send a self-addressed, stamped envelope and include a note if you're interested in fan club info!

17

Michael Chang

Super Stats

➤ Full name: Michael Te Pei Chang
➤ Birth date: February 22, 1972
➤ Birthplace: Hoboken, New Jersey
➤ Height: 5'8"
➤ Family: dad, Joe, and mom, Betty, are both chemists; older brother, Carl
➤ Interests and hobbies: fishing, raising tropical fish, studying the Bible
➤ Turned pro: 1988
➤ First great victory: winning the 1989 French Open by beating world champion Ivan Lendl and then Stefan Edberg. He was the youngest ever to win the tournament, and the first American to win it in 34 years.

*W*ith a string of "youngest ever" accolades already under his belt, tennis pro Michael Chang is steamin' these days. Dedicated and driven, Michael knows what it takes to win. He says the main ingredient in the formula is "hard work," and he also believes that his strong faith in God helps him to get where he wants to go—and that's straight up!

So You Want to Know —

What Michael wanted to be when he grew up, before he turned to tennis? He considered many occupations, including veterinarian, pediatrician, oceanographer, and fisherman!

Notable Quote

"I always try my best....One of the biggest things I've learned is that there's no shortcut to success."

Michael Chang
c/o Advantage International
1025 Thomas Jefferson St. NW #450E
Washington, DC 20007

Kevin Costner

Super Stats

➤ Birth date: January 18, 1955
➤ Birthplace: Los Angeles
➤ Raised in: Southern California
➤ Family: He married his college girlfriend, Cindy, and they have two daughters and a son.
➤ Education: degree in marketing from California State University at Fullerton
➤ Getaway spot: a condo in the California Sierras
➤ Leisurely pursuits: canoeing, fishing

Cool Credits

➤ **Film highlights:** *Testament, Fandango, Silverado, American Flyers, The Untouchables, No Way Out, Bull Durham, Field of Dreams, Revenge, Dances with Wolves* (which he also directed and produced), *Robin Hood: Prince of Thieves, JFK, The Bodyguard*

So You Want to Know —

How Kevin feels about doing love scenes? Nervous! Being a devoted family man for nearly two decades, he worries about how those steamy scenes will affect his home life.

Notable Quote

"I'm not that smart a person, not that forward a thinker. I have instincts for things and a great love for film."

A major Hollywood hunk today, Kevin had no ambitions to act until the day he read a chapter about film financing in a textbook in college. That was all it took, and he was on his way, starting out in community theater. He was unsure of himself at first, but it didn't take long for Kevin's natural confidence to come out, taking him to the top on the big screen!

Kevin Costner
c/o Tig Productions
4000 Warner Blvd.
Burbank, CA 91522

Cindy Crawford

▼▼▼▼▼▼▼▼▼▼▼▼▼▼▼▼▼▼▼▼▼▼▼▼

*T*he valedictorian of her high school class, Cindy won a scholarship to exclusive Northwestern University in the Chicago suburb of Evanston. There, she majored in engineering but also did small modeling jobs downtown. She modeled in catalogs for the Marshall Fields department stores before being referred to the Elite modeling agency. That's when she began to get so many modeling assignments that she had to put her engineering degree on hold. Cindy came on slow as a high-fashion face, but now she's as hot as any model can get!

Super Stats

➤ Birth date: February 20, 1967
➤ Born and raised in: DeKalb, Illinois
➤ Hair/eye color: brown/brown
➤ Height: 5'9-1/2"
➤ Family: Her parents separated when Cindy was 14. Her older sister is a teacher, and her younger sister recently graduated from college. Cindy is married to actor Richard Gere.
➤ First big break: making the cover of *Vogue* magazine

➤ Fave fashion shoot: in the Himalayas in India for British *Vogue*
➤ Modeling plus: has the most famous beauty mark in the business—the mole above her lip. Her first modeling agency wanted her to remove it, but she refused.
➤ Future goals: to have kids and maybe to finish college and start her own business

Career Coups

➤ had appeared on approximately 200 magazine covers by the time she was 23
➤ a host on MTV's "House of Style"
➤ Prince's song "Cindy C." is named after her
➤ at 23 grabbed the "brass ring" of modeling, becoming a Revlon Girl

So You Want to Know —

How Cindy maintains her gorgeous face and figure? She steams her face over hot water every morning, drinks lots of water, and goes to the gym regularly.

Notable Quote

"It's easy to identify your self-worth with the way you look....This is something all women live with, but for a model it's constant criticism."

Cindy Crawford
c/o Elite Model Management Corp.
111 E. 22nd St.
New York, NY 10010

Tom Cruise

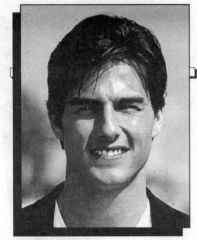

One of the movies' top guns, Tom has the survival instinct! He has a passion for fast cars, and he has raced professionally as well as in *Days of Thunder*, the movie that was his idea and in which he met his second wife, Australian actress Nicole Kidman. While in racing school, Tom was a straight-A student, proving he's a winner off-screen as well as on!

So You Want to Know —

How he let Nicole know he wanted to marry her? He left a big diamond ring under her pillow!

Super Stats

➤ Full name: Thomas Cruise Mapother III
➤ Birth date: July 3, 1962
➤ Birthplace: Syracuse, New York
➤ Raised in: many places, including New Jersey, Ohio, Kentucky, and Canada
➤ Height: 5'9"
➤ Obscure fact: Around the time Tom was filming *The Color of Money*, he wore an earring for good luck, a diamond given to him by his grandmother.

Cool Credits

➤ **Film:** a bit part in *Endless Love,* starring roles in *Taps, Risky Business, All the Right Moves, Top Gun, Legend, The Color of Money, Cocktail, Rain Man, Days of Thunder, Born on the Fourth of July, Far and Away*

Notable Quote

"Racing is like acting—just another chance for public humiliation! They both challenge you physically and mentally. You can't just go in and put your foot to the floor and expect to win. You have to think it out."

Tom Cruise
c/o PMK
955 S. Carrillo Dr. #200
Los Angeles, CA 90048

Johnny Depp

Dangerously handsome Johnny Depp left Florida to try his luck in Los Angeles in 1983. But he wasn't setting out to be an actor. He figured he was going to make his mark on the world as a musician. But short on cash, Johnny went to an acting audition, where he landed a part in the movie *A Nightmare on Elm Street*. His new career was off the ground!

So You Want to Know —

Johnny's most irrational fear? He's terrified of clowns!

Super Stats

➤ Full name: John Christopher Depp II
➤ Birth date: June 9, 1963
➤ Born in: Owensboro, Kentucky
➤ Family: dad, John C.; mom, Betty Sue Palmer
➤ Early bands he was in: The Kids, which opened for Billy Idol; Rock City Angels

➤ Tattoos: a Cherokee Indian chief, a banner with the words "Betty Sue," and one other name, "Winona" (their romance may be over, but the tattoo remains!)
➤ Fave actors: Marlon Brando, James Dean
➤ Ultimate fantasy: to sail around the world and buy an island

Cool Credits

➤ **TV:** "21 Jump Street"
➤ **Film:** *A Nightmare on Elm Street, Platoon, Cry-Baby, Edward Scissorhands, The Arrowtooth Waltz*

Notable Quote

"I'm an old-fashioned guy. I want a normal life, marriage, and kids. I want to be an old man with a beer belly and sit on the porch and look at the lake."

Johnny Depp
c/o ICM
8899 Beverly Blvd.
Los Angeles, CA 90048

Shannen Doherty

Super Stats

➤ Birth date: April 12, 1971
➤ Birthplace: Memphis, Tennessee
➤ Grew up in: Los Angeles
➤ Family: dad, Tom; mom, Rosa; older brother, Sean
➤ Fave footwear: combat boots
➤ Transportation: a black BMW convertible

Cool Credits

➤ **TV:** starring roles on "Little House: A New Beginning," "Father Murphy," "Our House," "Beverly Hills, 90210"
➤ **Film:** small parts in *Nightshift* and *The Treasure of Green Piney*, larger roles in *Girls Just Want to Have Fun* and *Heathers*

So You Want to Know —

How Shannen got into acting? At eight and a half, she went to watch a friend audition for a production of *Snow White*. When the director noticed her and asked her to try out, she did—and won one of the lead roles!

*P*laying Brenda Walsh, Shannen takes her job on "Beverly Hills, 90210" seriously. She has strong feelings about just how her character should be portrayed, and she lets those feelings be known on the set. It's obvious that her fans appreciate her hard work!

Notable Quote

"I made a decision that no matter how badly I wanted a job, I'd only play characters who had something going for them. I'd rather starve than compromise."

Shannen Doherty
"Beverly Hills, 90210"
P.O. Box 5600
Beverly Hills, CA 90209

Emilio Estevez

Super Stats

➤ Birth date: May 12, 1962
➤ Birthplace: New York City
➤ Raised in: Malibu, California
➤ Family: dad, actor Martin Sheen; mom, Janet, a film producer; brothers are Charlie Sheen (see page 53) and Ramon Estevez; younger sister, Renee Estevez
➤ Fave actors: James Dean, Robert DeNiro, Al Pacino, and his dad
➤ Fave pastime: working out

Cool Credits

➤ **TV:** *ABC Afterschool Special* "Seventeen Going on Nowhere"; TV movies *Nightmares* and *In the Custody of Strangers*
➤ **Film:** *Tex; The Outsiders; The Breakfast Club; Repo Man; St. Elmo's Fire; That Was Then, This Is Now* (also wrote); *Wisdom* (also wrote and directed); *Stakeout; Colors; Men at Work; Young Guns; Young Guns II*

Notable Quote

"I'm not a power-hungry human being, but I feel that I'm somewhat creative and that I have something to say."

E milio knew early on he would follow in his dad's footsteps. And although Sheen was a name his father took on when he began his own acting career, Emilio opted to use his birth name. And he's used it well. Not only has he starred in a string of films, he's also the youngest artist ever to have the triple credit of actor-writer-director on a film *(Wisdom)*.

So You Want to Know —

What Emilio considers one of his most embarrassing moments? Being voted king of his senior prom at Santa Monica High School!

Emilio Estevez
c/o InterTalent
131 South Rodeo Dr. #300
Beverly Hills, CA 90212

Linda Evangelista

▼▼▼▼▼▼▼▼▼▼▼▼▼▼▼▼▼▼▼▼▼▼▼

*B*y the age of 11, Linda was obsessed with fashion magazines (though she was also a straight-A student). She modeled for a local agency in Canada until, at 16, she entered a Miss Teen Niagara pageant. She didn't even place—but an Elite modeling agency scout was in the audience and gave Linda his card. It took her until she was 18 to get up the nerve to call, but it was a good move—obviously!

So You Want to Know —

When Linda reached superstar status? It happened in 1988, on the day she cut her hair short and caused an instant fashion sensation. The trend is still going strong, and there is even a wig sold in England called the "Evangelista"!

Super Stats

➤ Birth date: May 10, 1965
➤ Born and raised in: Saint Catharines, Ontario (Canada)
➤ Height: 5'9-1/2"
➤ Family: father, Thomas, is a General Motors employee; mother, Marisa, is a housewife
➤ Romance: married to Gerald Marie, one of the owners of the Elite modeling agency in Paris, since July 1987
➤ Best friend: Christy Turlington (more about Christy on page 61)

Notable Quote

"For so long it was always blond-haired, blue-eyed, button noses. That kind of model is only capable of one look. I'm versatile. I can do teenybopper, and I can do sophisticated and 45."

Linda Evangelista
c/o Elite Model Management Corp.
111 E. 22nd St.
New York, NY 10010

Jay Ferguson

Super Stats

➤ Full name: Jay Rowland Ferguson
➤ Birth date: July 25, 1974
➤ Born: Dallas, Texas
➤ Siblings: two younger half-brothers
➤ Extracurricular activities: backpacking, basketball, baseball, skiing, surfing, traveling, dancing
➤ Fave musicians: The Doors, Pink Floyd
➤ Fave TV shows: "Married… With Children" and "Cops"
➤ Fave food: seafood, pasta, and Mexican

Cool Credits

➤ **TV:** "The Outsiders," "Evening Shade"
➤ **Film:** Jay's actual debut was with his mother in a movie called *Drive-In,* when he was only 16 months old!

So You Want to Know ─

What Jay expects to be doing 10 years from now? Rather than acting, he feels it's more likely that he'll be writing and making music full time.

Notable Quote

"There's a time in your life when you stop thinking like a child and start thinking like an adult. I think I'm starting to make that transition."

*T*V is not the only place where Jay excels! He's also busy with his band, The Blank. That's part of the expression of this great-looking guy's sensitive side. He became a major Jim Morrison fan during his time on "The Outsiders" and discovered a whole new side of life. He's now an avid poet and often turns his work into lyrics for his band.

Jay R. Ferguson
c/o "Evening Shade"
4024 Radford Ave.
Building 5, Suite 104
Studio City, CA 91604

Jennie Garth

□ □

*L*ike her "Beverly Hills, 90210" cohort Luke Perry (found on page 43), Jennie grew up on a farm. When she was 13, her family moved to Phoenix, and that took some getting used to. The new girl in school had to learn to adapt to a whole new life-style in the city. Jennie began dance classes, and she excelled so quickly that she got up enough courage to enter a few teen beauty contests. In one of the pageants, Jennie was noticed by a talent scout and encouraged to get into acting. Though it hasn't been easy, she has had enough charm and talent to take her to the top!

Cool Credits

➤ **TV:** *Magical World of Disney* series, "A Brand New Life"; guest appearance on "Growing Pains"; "Beverly Hills, 90210"; Disney TV movies *Just Perfect* and *Teen Angel Returns* (Jason Priestley, found on page 46, was the angel!)

So You Want to Know —

Jennie's secret ambitions? Not only to continue acting, but also to own a farm and a horse, and, in the not-too-distant future, to get married!

Super Stats

➤ Birth date: April 3, 1972
➤ Birthplace: Urbana, Illinois
➤ Moved to: Phoenix, Arizona at 13
➤ Height: 5'5"
➤ Family: dad, John; mom, Carolyn; three older brothers and three older sisters
➤ Fave sports: horseback riding, tennis, dancing
➤ Interests: environmental and animal rights issues
➤ Fave way to dress: soft and loose, with little flowers
➤ Fave band: Rolling Stones
➤ Fave food: Mexican
➤ Fave colors: greens and reds
➤ Ideal date: a picnic in the park
➤ Pets: a dog (Sasha)
➤ Nicest thing she's done lately: made the down payment on her parents' new home

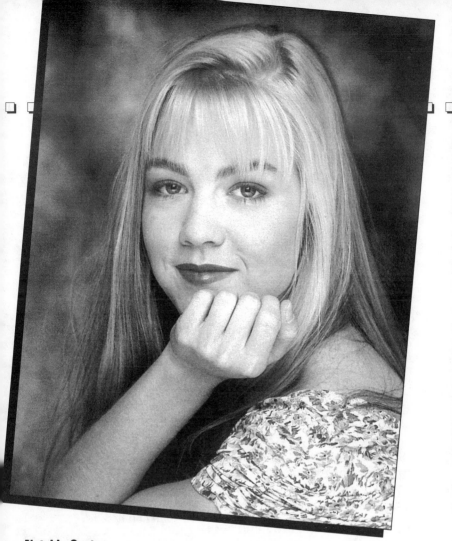

Notable Quote

"Living in a small town and coming from a very tight and close family instilled a lot of standards that I need to live up to."

• •

Jennie Garth
"Beverly Hills, 90210"
P.O. Box 5600
Beverly Hills, CA 90209

Send a self-addressed, stamped envelope and include a note if you're interested in fan club info!

• •

Balthazar Getty

Super Stats

➤ Full name: Paul Balthazar Getty
➤ Birth date: January 22, 1975
➤ Birthplace: Los Angeles
➤ Family: dad, Paul; mom, Gisela; sister, Anna
➤ Interests: drawing and painting, making videos, rock climbing
➤ Fave food: vegetarian

Notable Quote

"I've never felt like I had to do anything to fit in. I do whatever I feel is right."

Cool Credits

➤ **TV:** Steven Spielberg's Showtime production of "Turn of the Screw"
➤ **Film:** *Lord of the Flies, My Heroes Have Always Been Cowboys, Young Guns II, The Pope Must Diet, December, Where the Day Takes You, Red Hot*

*T*hough he's a private kind of guy, Balthazar comes on strong on-screen, a place he's been proving himself since he was 14. That was when he won one of two lead roles in the movie *Lord of the Flies* and went to Jamaica for filming. Since then, he's been dreaming of the time he can return to the islands and chill under a palm tree. For now he's too busy making movies to get away.

So You Want to Know —

About Balthazar's roots? The great grandson of the late oil billionaire J. Paul Getty, Balthazar gets his Irish heritage from that side of the family. He's also half German (from his mother's side), and he can speak that language fluently.

Balthazar Getty
c/o Triad
10100 Santa Monica Blvd.
16th Floor
Los Angeles, CA 90067

Amy Grant

So You Want to Know —

How Amy found God? She was a 15-year-old typical teen when a boy invited her to his Bible study class: "The guy who asked me to go was so cute that I thought I'd go to the meeting and get him to fall in love with me! Instead, I encountered the Bible in a way that helped me take care of my insides."

*A*my Grant is a powerhouse of feeling who deserves to be heard. She wrote the deeply felt love song "Baby, Baby" especially for her infant daughter, Millie. It was a pop hit, and she continues to stay near the top of the pop lists. This star's vocal abilities are so truly heavenly that four young nuns were once inspired to scale the security fence around Amy's home just to get her autograph!

Amy Grant
c/o Friends of Amy
P. O. Box 50701
Nashville, TN 37205

Super Stats

➤ Birth date: November 25, 1960
➤ Born and raised in: Nashville, Tennessee
➤ Family: married to guitarist Gary Chapman, and they have two children, Millie and Matt (a third one is due in November 1992!)
➤ Began guitar: at 13
➤ Thing she does best: cook spaghetti

Cool Tunes

➤ **Album highlights:** *Amy Grant, Age to Age, The Collection, Lead Me On, Unguarded, Heart in Motion*

Notable Quote

"I've got something good to say. It makes me want a lot of people to hear it."

Brian Austin Green

Notable Quote

"If you're not enjoying what you're doing, you shouldn't be doing it."

Playing school DJ David Silver in "Beverly Hills, 90210" comes easily for Brian. Besides being a dynamite drummer, he loves to strut his stuff onstage with his own band. He's also earth-aware. Besides being a conscientious consumer and dedicated recycler, Brian's involved in many environmental issues. Obviously, having him on the planet is a big plus—in more ways than one!

Super Stats

➤ Birth date: July 15, 1973
➤ Born and raised in: North Hollywood, California
➤ Family: dad, George, a drummer; mom, Joyce, Brian's manager; older half-brother, Keith; older half-sister, Laurie
➤ Fave musicians: Bell Biv Devoe, Big Daddy Kane, Hammer (see page 34), Bobby Brown
➤ Fave food: Italian, Mexican
➤ Transportation: a black Ford Bronco
➤ On girls: "I like a girl with a great personality and a good sense of humor...."

Cool Credits

➤ **TV:** debuted on "Knots Landing"; "Beverly Hills, 90210"
➤ **Film:** *Kid, Kickboxer II, An American Summer*

So You Want to Know —

Brian's favorite acting experience? Playing a rebel boy in the movie *Kid*—the character was a switch for him after playing only nice guys!

Brian Austin Green
"Beverly Hills, 90210"
P.O. Box 5600
Beverly Hills, CA 90209

Richard Grieco

*I*f fate hadn't intervened, Richard might have been a football star instead of a hot young actor. A high school football All-American, he attended Central Connecticut University on an athletic scholarship. After three knee injuries, Richard had to give up his football dreams. He later won a national contest, "The Best Faces of the '80s," and that was the start of a whole new career!

Notable Quote

"There's a fine line between struggle and success, and I'm not afraid to walk that line."

Super Stats

➤ Birth date: March 23, 1967
➤ Birthplace: Watertown, New York
➤ Fave sports: hockey, lacrosse, football
➤ Other interests: growing roses, hanging out in cafes, writing poetry, and working out (which he does religiously four times a week)
➤ Fave actors: Marlon Brando, Robert DeNiro

Cool Credits

➤ **TV:** "One Life To Live," "21 Jump Street," "Booker"
➤ **Film:** *If Looks Could Kill, Mobsters*

Richard Grieco
c/o Susan Culley & Assoc.
132A Lasky Dr.
Beverly Hills, CA 90212

Hammer

□ □

Watch out! It's Hammer time! This is one incredible dude, to say the least. Rapper *extraordinaire* Hammer started out on the streets and saw a very mean way of life early on. He was involved in robberies, gang fights, and drugs, and plenty of his friends went by the wayside before Hammer realized he'd better make his break. And break he did. He came clean in a major way, and now his message is pure positivity. Hammer is a man who cares. For instance, when Hammer dolls became available, he insisted that 10 percent of every sale go to his Help the Children Foundation and another $50,000 to New York's Hale House, a home for crack-addicted and AIDS-infected babies.

Hammer has said right from the start that he had wanted to do rap in a different way. He wanted a strong, positive message as well as "a show that was entertaining, a spectacle. And most of all, I wanted to be successful." Being the kind of incredible person Hammer is—rad rapper, dynamite dancer, and all-around really great guy—it's no wonder he got his wish!

Cool Credits

➤ **Albums:** *Let's Get It Started, Please Hammer Don't Hurt 'Em* (which has sold more than 20 million copies, making it the biggest-selling rap record of all time), *Too Legit to Quit*
➤ **Videos:** "Please Hammer Don't Hurt 'Em—The Movie," which received a Grammy nomination for best long-form video; "Hammer Time"

So You Want to Know —

What Hammer was like as a kid? Believe it or not, until his last year of high school, he was super short! And to make matters worse, he had, as he puts it, "a big wad of a head. A little skinny body and a big ol' man's head." He painfully recalls that kids used to shout out at him, "Come here, ol' Big Head Boy!"

Super Stats

➤ Real name: Stanley Kirk Burrell
➤ Nickname given to him by the Oakland Athletics: Little Hammer
➤ Birth date: March 29
➤ Born and raised in: Oakland, California
➤ Hair/eye color: black/brown
➤ Height: 5'11"
➤ About his eyesight: It's just fine—he wears glasses purely for decorative effect!
➤ Family: Hammer is one of nine kids raised by a single mom; he has a small daughter named Akeiba Monique, about whom he says, "She's my everything."
➤ Military experience: spent some time in the Navy
➤ Fave musicians: James Brown, Rick James, Prince, Marvin Gaye
➤ First-love sport: baseball
➤ First serious rap effort: formed a religious rap duo called The Holy Ghost Boys

Notable Quote

"There is good in everyone. But in many kids, it's being suffocated."

➤ Awards and honors: too many to list them all! In 1990 alone he won five American Music Awards and three MTV awards, plus an NAACP Image Award and a Billboard Award, both for Best Rap Artist. The list goes on and on!

Hammer
c/o Capitol Records
810 Seventh Ave.
New York, NY 10019

or

Bust It Productions
80 Swan Way, Suite 130
Oakland, CA 94621

Hammer Official Fan Club:
The Hammer Posse
P.O. Box 884988
San Francisco, CA 94188

Ethan Hawke

Cute and way cool Ethan Hawke has been hot for acting ever since high school, when he first appeared in some school productions. He later studied acting at Carnegie-Mellon University in Pittsburgh, and he got more training and a little highbrow culture when he studied acting in England.

Notable Quote

"The trouble with having success young is that I'm not clear about what I want. And I'm never going to get it until I know what it is."

So You Want to Know —

Where Ethan has learned the most about acting? From actor Jeremy Irons, with whom he worked in *Waterland.* Ethan says, "Until I worked with him, I had no idea how much I didn't know."

Super Stats

➤ Full name: Ethan Green Hawke
➤ Birth date: November 6, 1971
➤ Birthplace: Austin, Texas
➤ Current residence: New York City
➤ Authors he loves: J. D. Salinger, Henry Miller
➤ Fave novel: *Catcher in the Rye*
➤ Fave hang-out clothes: really old jeans with holes, high-tops, and a beat-up sweater
➤ Hates: doing interviews

Cool Credits

➤ **Film:** *Explorers, Dead Poets Society, Dad, White Fang, Mystery Date, A Midnight Clear, Waterland, Rich in Love*

Ethan Hawke
c/o PMK
1776 Broadway
8th Floor
New York, NY 10019

Janet Jackson

*L*ike her eight older brothers and sisters, Janet Jackson has been in the spotlight most of her life! By the time she was seven, Janet had already performed onstage with the Jackson 5. She wrote her very first song, "Fantasy," when she was eight. At 16, she cut her first album, and at 20 she had a double-platinum LP and thousands of fans all over the world.

Super Stats

➤ Birth date: May 16, 1967
➤ Birthplace: Gary, Indiana
➤ Raised in: Encino, California
➤ Pets: dogs, chimpanzees, rats, snakes, a llama, and a giraffe—to name only a few!
➤ Accessory trademark: her house-key earring
➤ Burning ambition: to own a king cobra

Cool Credits

➤ **Albums:** *Janet Jackson, Dream Street, Control, Rhythm Nation 1814*

Notable Quote

"My parents were very strict when we were growing up. It was really just our music and our work....We missed out on our childhood, getting to know what really goes on out there."

So You Want to Know —

About Janet's first profession-al appearance? It took place in Las Vegas when, at seven, she got up onstage and performed with her brothers, The Jackson 5. She finished up with her Mae West imperson-ation (which she says she can't do anymore), and then got a standing ovation!

Janet Jackson
c/o Levine Schneider
8730 Sunset Blvd.
6th Floor
Los Angeles, CA 90069

Magic Johnson

▼▼▼▼▼▼▼▼▼▼▼▼▼

Super Stats

➤ Full name: Earvin Johnson, Jr.
➤ Birth date: August 14, 1959
➤ Born and raised in: Lansing, Michigan
➤ Height: 6'9"
➤ Family: He married his high school sweetheart, Cookie, and they have a young son.
➤ Education: two years at Michigan State as a communications major
➤ Loves: playing music on his boom box, dancing, helping kids
➤ Cool career coup: received the most lucrative and longest-running contract ever offered in sports history: $25 million over 25 years

Notable Quote

"EJ the DJ was born to make people have a good time."

Magic Johnson became a professional ball player when the Los Angeles Lakers snagged him from his college team, Michigan State. He put major "magic" into the game until his retirement at the end of 1991. He left the team when he learned he had contracted the AIDS virus. Since then, he has worked tirelessly to inform kids about how to lessen their chances of contracting the disease.

So You Want to Know —

How Earvin, Jr., came to be known as "Magic"? A Lansing, Michigan, sportswriter hung that nickname on the three-time All-Stater after he scored 36 points, got 18 rebounds, and handed out 16 assists, *all in one game*—while still in high school!

Magic Johnson
c/o Los Angeles Lakers
P.O. Box 10
Inglewood, CA 90301

also:
P.O. Box 32
Inglewood, CA 90312

Michael Jordan

*T*here was a time when basketball superstar Michael Jordan was so short, the idea of playing pro ball wasn't worth considering. But during his junior year he began to sprout, and it was obvious his time on the court was coming.

Michael's college career was interrupted when he was drafted by the Chicago Bulls, and he's been with them ever since!

Notable Quote

"Michael Jordan isn't caught up in the flashy life.... He knows where he came from and what it took to get him where he is right now. I haven't changed my personality at all."

So You Want to Know —

About Michael's growth spurt? Although he had only grown to 5'11" by the time he turned 16, Michael shot up to 6'6" by the time he was a senior.

Super Stats

➤ Birth date: February 17, 1963
➤ Birthplace: Wilmington, North Carolina
➤ Current residence: Northbrook, Illinois
➤ Education: accepted a scholarship to the University of North Carolina before he'd even finished high school; dropped out in 1984 to join the Chicago Bulls, who offered him a 7-figure, 5-year contract
➤ Off-court endeavors: visits schools and basketball clinics
➤ Special award: received a gold medal in the 1984 Olympics in Los Angeles as co-captain of the Olympic basketball team

Michael Jordan
c/o Chicago Bulls
980 N. Michigan Ave.
Suite 1600
Chicago, IL 60611-4501

Michael Jordan Fan Club
c/o Nike Promotions
One Bowerman Drive
Beaverton, OR 97005

Madonna

*T*he girl with a thousand faces! That's Madonna, all right, always changing her look, coming on with a new style, turning heads, and opting for the unpredictable. One thing always remains the same, and that's her dynamic drive to outdo herself and get the best out of her talent! From the time she was a small girl, Madonna knew where she was going and what she had to do to get there. She was completely dedicated to all her dance classes, and she also studied piano. To achieve the fame and fortune she craved, Madonna had to make a lot of sacrifices, one of which was leaving her hairdresser boyfriend back in Michigan when she made the big move to New York. And though Madonna's the kind of girl that everybody feels strongly about—for good or for bad—one thing is obvious: her amazing "blond ambition" has taken her to the dizzying heights of worldwide superstardom!

So You Want to Know —

What Madonna collected as a kid? She had a large stash of religious artifacts, including many rosaries. Her favorite was a turquoise one her grandma gave her, which she wore all the time as a necklace.

Notable Quote

"I'm ambitious, but if I weren't as talented as I am ambitious I'd be a gross monstrosity. I'm not surprised by my success because it feels natural."

Super Stats

➤ Full name: Madonna Louise Veronica Ciccone
➤ Birth date: August 16, 1958
➤ Born and raised in: Detroit, Michigan
➤ Hair/eye color: naturally brown and usually blond/blue
➤ Family: father, Silvio (known as Tony); mother, Madonna, who died when Madonna was six and whom she says she still misses more than anybody in the world. Madonna has seven brothers and sisters (Anthony, Martin, Paula, Christopher, Melanie, Jennifer, Mario).
➤ Siblings' nickname for Madonna: Squeeze
➤ Early ambition: to be a nun

► Education: three semesters as a fine arts major at the University of Michigan

► Early band work: sang and played drums with The Breakfast Club in New York City

► Other work: waitressed at Dunkin' Donuts on Broadway when she first got to the Big Apple

► Causes she cares about: deeply involved in AIDS benefit work; has also made extremely large contributions to cancer research and programs for terminally ill children

► Guy watching: "Dark, brooding men with tough tempers"

► Fave food: Italian

► Fave movie: *Murmur of the Heart*

► Fave actresses: Carole Lombard, Marilyn Monroe

► Fave musicians: Ella Fitzgerald, Sam Cooke, Sarah Vaughan, Aretha Franklin, B. B. King, Joni Mitchell

► Fave authors: Henry Miller, James Joyce, D. H. Lawrence

► Strongest traits: ambition and self-confidence

Cool Credits

► **Film:** *Desperately Seeking Susan* (her debut), *Shanghai Surprise, Who's That Girl?, Truth or Dare* (autobiographical documentary), *Dick Tracy, A League of Their Own*

► **Albums:** *Madonna, Like a Virgin, Immaculate Collection, Like a Prayer, True Blue, The Royal Box, Who's That Girl?, Vision Quest* (movie soundtrack), *You Can Dance, I'm Breathless* (music from and inspired by the film *Dick Tracy*)

Madonna
The Official Madonna Fan Club
8491 Sunset Blvd. #485
Los Angeles, CA 90069

Marky Mark

Being the little brother of Donnie Wahlberg of New Kids on the Block wasn't that easy for Marky Mark until he hit it big himself. Now, as the front man of his own group, he's got all the fame he'll ever need. He was briefly a member of the New Kids, but he decided to forge his own path.

Notable Quote

"I'm not trying to brag about hard times and that I'm some big, tough guy. There are a lot of people like me. I just survived the streets."

So You Want to Know —

Why Marky quit the New Kids? "I didn't have the dedication to go to school all day and then rehearse all night," he says. Also, Marky liked the sounds of hip-hop music. "The style of music [of the New Kids] wasn't really me. When we did our second song, a love song, I just said, 'I can't do this.' I didn't fit."

Super Stats

➤ Full Name: Mark Robert Wahlberg
➤ Birth date: June 5, 1971
➤ Born and raised in: Dorchester, Massachusetts
➤ Fave musicians: Main Event
➤ First award: named Best New Rap Act at the 1991 Boston Music Awards
➤ Fave movie: *The Adventures of Ford Fairlane*
➤ Little-known fact: talks in his sleep

Cool Credits

➤ **Album:** Marky Mark and the Funky Bunch had three hit records from their debut LP, *Music for the People*

Marky Mark and the Funky Bunch
P. O. Box 207
Quincy, MA 02269

Luke Perry

Super Stats

➤ Full name: Coy Luther Perry III
➤ Birth date: October 11, 1966
➤ Family: father, Coy, and his mom, Ann, divorced when Luke was six; brother, Tom; sister, Amy; Luke's stepfather, Steve Bennett; stepsister, Emily
➤ High school title: Biggest Flirt
➤ Fave music: opera, especially *Carmen,* and '50s rock 'n' roll
➤ Fave foods: steak and potatoes
➤ Social causes: Greenpeace and other environmental issues
➤ Girl watching: "Looks don't matter that much to me. "

Cool Credits

➤ **TV:** "Loving," "Another World," "Beverly Hills, 90210"
➤ **Film:** *Terminal Bliss; Scorchers; Buffy, The Vampire Slayer*

So You Want to Know —

How Luke got that scar on his right eyebrow? He was goofing off in a bowling alley and got pushed into a soda machine that had a mean jagged edge!

Notable Quote

"I believe you have to live your life with a certain degree of madness, and mine has just a little more than most folks."

Like his character Dylan McKay on the hot television series "Beverly Hills, 90210," Luke is somewhat of a loner. A streak of his originality surfaced when he chose a pet—a black pig named Jerry Lee, after rocker Jerry Lee Lewis. "He looks just like Elvis," Luke says of his animal companion. "Big pork-chop sideburns. He's got charisma." And so does Luke—obviously!

Luke Perry
"Beverly Hills, 90210"
P.O. Box 5600
Beverly Hills, CA 90209

River Phoenix

Notable Quote

"I've learned that if you can't get it all together to accomplish this thing called 'peace,' you at least do your part in your own life, because that's where you can make an immediate difference."

E arthy and intellectual, River is involved in many important issues of the day. He comes from a family that's been caring about issues since the '60s, when his parents lived an alternative lifestyle (and basically still do). The close-knit Phoenix clan live on 20 acres of land in Florida, where River likes to stay—except when Hollywood calls, of course!

Super Stats

➤ Full name: River Jude Phoenix
➤ Nickname: Rio
➤ Birth date: August 23, 1970
➤ Birthplace: Madras, Oregon
➤ Family: dad, John; mom, Arlyn; sisters are Liberty, Summer, and Rainbow; brother, Leaf
➤ Fave authors: Kahlil Gibran, Aldous Huxley
➤ Fave movie: *Brazil*
➤ Fave food: anything that's not meat—River's a vegetarian!

Cool Credits

➤ **Film:** *Stand By Me, Little Nikita, A Night in the Life of Jimmy Reardon, The Mosquito Coast, Running on Empty, Indiana Jones and the Last Crusade, I Love You to Death, Dogfight, My Own Private Idaho, Sneakers*

So You Want to Know —

The name of River's band? It's Aleka's Attic. The album they played on, *Tame Yourself,* also includes cuts by the B-52's, Jeff Beck, Erasure, Jane Wiedlin, k. d. lang, Belinda Carlisle, and others.

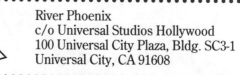

River Phoenix
c/o Universal Studios Hollywood
100 Universal City Plaza, Bldg. SC3-1
Universal City, CA 91608

Paulina Porizkova

*P*aulina, one of the hottest models around, remembers when she was so homely that two boys once dumped a bucket of paint over her head, saying she deserved to be covered up. She's been modeling successfully since she was 15, and she has always made it clear that modeling is just a job for her. Extremely intelligent, Paulina has little patience for the "ditzy" model stereotype.

Notable Quote

"My private life is my private life, and my work is my work. Work is what I have to do to earn my money, and my private life has nothing whatsoever to do with it."

So You Want to Know —

What Paulina's interested in? She speaks six languages, plays classical piano, paints in oils and colored charcoals, and is writing her autobiography.

Super Stats

➤ Birth date: April 9, 1965
➤ Birthplace: Czechoslovakia
➤ Raised in: Czechoslovakia and Sweden
➤ Height: 5'10"
➤ Family: father and mother are both doctors; a younger brother; she's married to singer Ric Ocasek
➤ Fave authors: Dickens and Dostoevsky
➤ Philosophy of life: "Just a little bit of humor, intelligence, and dignity, and you get along fine."

Career Coups

➤ Appeared in the movies *Anna* and *Her Alibi* (with Tom Selleck)
➤ Appeared in the Cars' music video "Drive"

Paulina Porizkova
c/o Elite Model Management Corp.
111 E. 22nd St.
New York, NY 10010

Jason Priestley

❏ ❏

*J*ason was still in diapers when he made his first professional appearance. He was featured in a commercial, crying his eyes out, and the actress holding him in the scene was his mother, Sharon! He did a string of commercials before landing the lead—at eight—in the Canadian TV movie *Stacey.* In 1987, Jason moved to Los Angeles, and the rest is history! These days he's breaking hearts in his native Canada as well as in the U.S. as sexy and sensitive Brandon Walsh on the top teen show "Beverly Hills, 90210."

Jason confesses he's not as picture-perfect as his character Brandon. He likes to stay up late, hates to shave, and has the constant urge to seek out thrills and chills wherever he can find 'em. He loves winding it out on a fast motorcycle and has gone bungee jumping with his best buddy and co-star Luke Perry (see Luke on page 43). Maybe it was Jason's grandfather (who was a circus acrobat) who passed along the wild blood, because Jason's definitely got his share!

Notable Quote

"It's not about how much money I make. It's to have the freedom to create and to be."

So You Want to Know —

About Jason's filmmaking credits? After two of his friends died in drunk-driving accidents in high school, Jason and another buddy made a movie. Called *One Single Raindrop*, it's a short feature about the dangers of drinking and driving. They wrote, directed, produced, acted in, and edited the whole thing themselves!

Super Stats

➤ Full name: Jason Bradford Priestley
➤ Birth date: August 28, 1967
➤ Birthplace: Vancouver, British Columbia (Canada)
➤ Hair/eye color: light brown/hazel-blue
➤ Height: 5'9"
➤ Family: dad, Lorne; mom, Sharon; sister, Justine, who lives in London
➤ Fave singer: Elvis Costello
➤ Fave TV shows: "Married… With Children" and CNN news programs
➤ Fave movies: *The Killing Fields, A Clockwork Orange*
➤ Fave actors: Robert Duvall, Al Pacino, Dennis Hopper, James Woods
➤ Fave sports: ice hockey, rugby, downhill skiing
➤ Transportation: an Alfa Romeo, but he loves motorcycles, too!

Cool Credits

➤ **TV:** appearances on "21 Jump Street," "MacGyver," and "Quantum Leap"; starring roles in "Sister Kate" and, of course, "Beverly Hills, 90210"; TV movies: *Lies from Lotus Land, Nobody's Child,* and *Teen Angel* and *Teen Angel Returns* (for the Disney Channel)
➤ **Film:** *Watchers, The Boy Who Could Fly, Nowhere to Run*

Jason Priestley
"Beverly Hills, 90210"
P.O. Box 5600
Beverly Hills, CA 90209

Send a self-addressed, stamped envelope and include a note if you're interested in fan club info!

47

Keanu Reeves

*U*sually found playing some kind of quirky character, Keanu is now beginning to show an exciting new range in his abilities. He's always attracted fans from every age group, and he'll undoubtedly continue to do so as he matures into major romantic leading-man roles. Keep your eye on this guy—he's bound to steal the hearts of fans as well as film *femme fatales* every step of the way!

Notable Quote

"I don't look like a classic North American."

So You Want to Know —

What Keanu's first name means? His parents say it's Hawaiian for "cool breeze over a mountain."

Super Stats

➤ Full name: Keanu Charles Reeves
➤ Birth date: September 2, 1964
➤ Birthplace: Beirut, Lebanon
➤ Raised in: New York till he was six and then Toronto, Ontario (Canada)
➤ Early ambitions: to be a race car driver or an inventor
➤ First professional job: a Coca-Cola commercial, at 16
➤ Fave author: sci-fi novelist Philip K. Dick
➤ Fave music: the blues; Husker Du, The Ramones, The Pixies
➤ Fave sports: hockey and basketball

Cool Credits

➤ **Film highlights:** *River's Edge, Bill and Ted's Excellent Adventure, Bill and Ted's Bogus Journey, Dangerous Liaisons, Parenthood, I Love You to Death, Tune in Tomorrow, Point Break, My Own Private Idaho, Bram Stoker's Dracula*

Keanu Reeves
c/o PMK
955 S. Carrillo Dr. #200
Los Angeles, CA 90048

Julia Roberts

*M*ore than just a sweet Southern belle, leggy Julia Roberts became the hottest attraction in Hollywood when *Pretty Woman* opened. Besides her dazzling smile and her fresh appearance, Julia's known for her ability to get right down to raw emotions in her acting.

Notable Quote

"I feel proud of the work I've done, but I don't think I've achieved any sort of perfection in the realization of characters. You always say, 'Oh, I could have done that a little bit differently, or a little bit better.' "

So You Want to Know —

Why Julia changed her name from Julie (which is on her birth certificate) to Julia? When she came to Hollywood, she discovered there was already an actress named Julie Roberts, so she needed to choose something different.

Super Stats

➤ Birth date: October 28, 1967
➤ Born and raised in: Smyrna, Georgia
➤ Family: dad, Walter, died in 1976; mom, Betty Motes; sister, Lisa; brother, Eric
➤ Earliest ambition: to be a veterinarian
➤ Hobby: needlepoint
➤ Tattoo: a tiny heart on her back
➤ Achievements: two Oscar nominations and two Golden Globe awards, all for *Pretty Woman* and *Steel Magnolias*

Cool Credits

➤ **TV:** "Crime Story"; the HBO movie *Baja California*
➤ **Film:** *Satisfaction, Mystic Pizza, Blood Red* (with brother Eric), *Steel Magnolias, Pretty Woman, Flatliners, Sleeping with the Enemy, Dying Young, Hook*

Julia Roberts
c/o Nancy Seltzer
6220 Del Valle Drive
Los Angeles, CA 90048

Axl Rose

Super Stats

➤ Real name: William Rose
➤ Birth date: February 6, 1962
➤ Raised in: Lafayette, Indiana
➤ Fave singer: Frank Sinatra
➤ Musical influences: Aerosmith, New York Dolls
➤ Other band he's been in: L.A. Guns
➤ Pet peeve: when somebody calls Guns N' Roses' music heavy metal
➤ Worst habit: he's late for everything

Notable Quote

"Don't give up, and make sure to cover all your bases. And try not to make too many enemies."

The bad boy of hard rock, Guns N' Roses front man Axl Rose comes from a deeply troubled background (he was abandoned by his real father), and that painful time has given him inspiration for his music. In 1991, he ended his 15-year partnership with band mate Izzy Stradlin, and he saw his two newest LP efforts fly straight up the charts—keep watching for his latest developments!

Cool Tunes

➤ **Albums:** *Appetite for Destruction; Days of Thunder; Guns N' Roses Lies; Lean on Me; Nobody's Child—Romanian Angel Appeal; Use Your Illusion, I & II*

So You Want to Know —

About Axl's name? Though his real first name is William, he began calling himself W. Axl, after the name of a band he was once in. When he signed with the David Geffen Company, he legally changed his name to W. Axl Rose, and he now goes by Axl Rose.

Axl Rose
c/o Guns N' Roses
David Geffen Co.
9130 Sunset Blvd.
Los Angeles, CA 90069

Winona Ryder

*W*insome and irresistible Winona Ryder came into the world in Winona, Minnesota. The town was supposedly named after a legendary Indian princess, so Winona's parents decided to name their new daughter after the princess. After living in Oregon for a while, the family moved to San Francisco, where Winona got interested in acting. And she's been at it ever since!

Super Stats

➤ Birth date: October 1971
➤ Birthplace: Winona, Minnesota
➤ Raised in: mostly in San Francisco, but also in Oregon and South America
➤ Other aspirations: to write a screenplay, and to study history and literature at Trinity College in Ireland
➤ Fave band: The Replacements
➤ Likes: traveling (Texas is one of her favorite places)
➤ Her idol: her character, Veronica, in *Heathers*

Cool Credits

➤ **Film:** *Lucas; Square Dance; Beetlejuice; 1969; Heathers; Great Balls of Fire; Welcome Home, Roxy Carmichael; Mermaids; Edward Scissorhands; Bram Stoker's Dracula; Night on Earth; The Age of Innocence*

So You Want to Know —

Who did Winona's wardrobe in *Beetlejuice*? As a matter of fact, she did! Most of the clothes she wore in that movie were her own.

Notable Quote

"I don't really worry about my looks, and I don't worry about getting old. Exterior beauty doesn't mean a lot to me."

Winona Ryder
c/o PMK
1776 Broadway, 8th Floor
New York, NY 10019

Claudia Schiffer

*S*ince she was discovered in a Düsseldorf club a few years ago, Claudia's become a major celebrity. Unlike many models, she isn't gossipy, doesn't act like a prima donna, and she arrives on time to her assignments. Claudia has graced the covers and pages of everything from leading fashion magazines to *Rolling Stone.*

So You Want to Know —

The conditions that Claudia puts on her fashion photo shoots? As one of the most sought-after models in the business, she's able to call the shots about what she will and won't do. For instance, she won't model lingerie, won't wear dark lipstick, and has the right to approve which photographers, hairstylists, and makeup artists she'll work with.

Notable Quote

"I'm making investments, but they're all for the future. I'm very German in that way. Everything is very well thought out."

Super Stats

➤ Birth date: August 16, 1970
➤ Birthplace: Rheinberg, Germany, near Düsseldorf
➤ Current residence: New York City
➤ Height: 5'10"
➤ Fave city: Paris
➤ Fave fashion look: a miniskirt or jeans with a cashmere sweater
➤ Romantic attachments: has a boyfriend, but won't say a thing about him!
➤ Interests: art, history, visiting museums, exercising, tennis
➤ Earlier aspiration: to be a lawyer

Claudia Schiffer
c/o Metropolitan Management
5 Union Square West
5th Floor
New York, NY 10003

Charlie Sheen

□ □ □ □ □ □ □ □ □ □ □ □   □ □

Super Stats

➤ Real name: Carlos Irwin Estevez
➤ Birth date: September 3, 1965
➤ Birthplace: New York City
➤ Family: dad, actor Martin Sheen; mom, Janet, a film producer; brothers Emilio (see page 25) and Ramon; sister, Renee
➤ Main passions: baseball, rollerball, and acting
➤ Fave movies: *Badlands* and *Apocalypse Now* (in which he was an extra)
➤ Childhood neighbors: Sean and Chris Penn, C. Thomas Howell, Rob and Chad Lowe

Cool Credits

➤ **Film highlights**: *Grizzly II—The Predator, Red Dawn, Major League, Lucas, Platoon, Young Guns, Wall Street, Hot Shots!*

So You Want to Know —

Why Charlie changed his name? His real first name is Carlos, but since he's hardly ever called that, his stage name would have been Charlie Estevez. He didn't like the way it sounded, so he took his dad's stage name, Sheen.

Notable Quote

"I've grown to trust my instincts, but not to where I'm cocky. There's a fine line between confidence and cockiness."

A guy who grew up in the film business, Charlie excelled as a shortstop in high school and might have ended up as a professional baseball player. But right after graduation he won a part in *Grizzly II—The Predator*, and his life took a different direction. With his striking good looks and his acting ability, Charlie is never out of work. In fact, he's a bona fide hot Hollywood hunk!

Charlie Sheen
c/o William Morris
151 El Camino
Beverly Hills, CA 90212

Christian Slater

■ ■ ■ ■ ■ ■ ■ ■ ■ ■ ■ ■ ■ ■ ■ ■ ■

C hristian's been acting practically since he was a baby, so he's had plenty of time to develop his talents—and it shows! He was introduced to his career at age seven when his casting-director mom gave him a small part in the soap "One Life to Live." When the cast and crew applauded that very first performance, he knew that he was headed for the bright lights. And now that he's there, he's one of the most brightly shining young stars around!

Super Stats

➤ Birth date: August 18, 1969
➤ Born and raised in: New York City
➤ Height: 5'9"
➤ Family: dad, Michael Hawkins, a stage actor; mom, Mary Jo Slater, a casting director
➤ Passions: acting, women, collecting *Star Wars* memorabilia, and sleeping in
➤ His own work he likes best: *Pump Up the Volume*
➤ First directing experience: a recent play in Los Angeles called *The Laughter Epidemic* to benefit the Pediatric AIDS Foundation
➤ Fave music: Seal, Frank Sinatra

➤ Signs autographs: "Safe sex from Christian Slater"
➤ Fave book: *Way of the Peaceful Warrior*

Cool Credits

➤ **Film:** *The Legend of Billie Jean* (his debut), *The Name of the Rose*, *Tucker: The Man and His Dream*, *Gleaming the Cube*, *Heathers*, *The Wizard*, *Young Guns II*, *Tales from the Dark Side—The Movie*, *Pump Up the Volume*, *Robin Hood: Prince of Thieves*, *Mobsters*, *Kuffs*, *Baboon Heart*

So You Want to Know —

If Christian's ever dressed up like a girl? He has! For a scene in *The Legend of Billie Jean*, he appeared in a dress, a wig, and lipstick.

Notable Quote

"I try not to regret anything I've done in the past. I do things to the extreme. I just do it now without risking anybody's life, particularly my own."

• •

Christian Slater
c/o Susan Culley & Assoc.
132A Lasky Dr.
Beverly Hills, CA 90212

• •

Will Smith

Super Stats

➤ Birth date: September 25, 1968
➤ Born and raised in: Philadelphia, Pennsylvania
➤ Height: 6'2"
➤ Family influences: Will says his dad was "always in my business," keeping him straight and making sure he didn't get into anything bad
➤ Hobbies: traveling, reading

Notable Quote

"Never try for luck. Always have a plan, and take your shot with that."

Cool Credits

➤ **Albums:** *DJ Jazzy Jeff and the Fresh Prince; Rock the House; I'm the Rapper, He's the DJ; And in This Corner…; Home Base*
➤ **TV:** "The Fresh Prince of Bel Air"
➤ **Film:** *Where the Day Takes You*

Will Smith has been a poetry man since he was a little kid. But it wasn't until he was a junior in high school, when he hooked up with DJ Jazzy Jeff, that things really started to take off. The duo turned their skills into an excellent music gig. Now, with his amazing success in music, TV, and movies, Will's a three-way wonder who won't quit!

So You Want to Know —

Where Will got the nickname "Fresh Prince"? When he was a schoolboy in Philadelphia, one of his teachers began calling him Prince Charming because that's exactly what he was! Later, when he began to get into rap, street friends dubbed Will the Fresh Prince, and the name stuck!

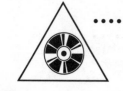

Will Smith
c/o "Fresh Prince of Bel Air"
NBC-TV
3000 W. Alameda
Burbank, CA 91523

Tori Spelling

As a little girl, Tori knew more about the business than most kids her age because her father was—and still is—a successful TV producer. When he became the producer for "Beverly Hills, 90210," Tori knew it was the perfect program for her. With her long list of acting credits and her talent, she was able to land the role of upscale Donna Martin.

Notable Quote

"It's not important to me where my friends come from or how much money they have. I'm friends with lots of different people, with different backgrounds and interests."

So You Want to Know —

If Tori's fashion sense is the same as her character Donna's? It's not! "She wears lots of short, tight stuff," says Tori. "I'm into looking casual…like jeans and T-shirts."

Super Stats

➤ Full name: Victoria Davey Spelling
➤ Birth date: May 16, 1973
➤ Birthplace: Los Angeles
➤ Raised in: Bel Air, California
➤ Family: dad, Aaron; mom, Candy; brother, Randy
➤ Fave books: horror novels
➤ Transportation: a champagne-colored BMW
➤ First ambition: to be a manicurist

Cool Credits

➤ **TV:** "Beverly Hills, 90210"; episodes of "The Love Boat," "T. J. Hooker," "Saved By the Bell," "Hotel," "Fantasy Island"
➤ **Film:** *Troop Beverly Hills*

Tori Spelling
c/o Rogers & Cowan
10000 Santa Monica Blvd.
Los Angeles, CA 90067

or

c/o "Beverly Hills, 90210"
P.O. Box 5600
Beverly Hills, CA 90209

Kiefer Sutherland

Although Kiefer looks and acts much like his renowned actor father, Donald, he's hardly spent any time with him at all, since the elder Sutherland moved to Hollywood when Kiefer was four. But he's definitely inherited the talent and has said he'd love to work with his dad! Kiefer has had to rely on himself to make it on his own, and that's a good thing. His impressive list of films proves he's got what it takes to be a success in Hollywood!

Super Stats

➤ Full name: Kiefer William Frederick Dempsey George Rufus Sutherland—or so he says!
➤ Birth date: 1967
➤ Raised in: Toronto and Ottawa, Ontario (Canada)
➤ Hair/eye color: dark blond/blue-green
➤ Height: 5'10"
➤ Family: dad, movie star Donald Sutherland; mom, stage actress Shirley Douglas; twin sister, Rachel (who's 6' tall!). His parents divorced when the twins were four.
➤ Romantic liaisons: was married to Camelia Kath, 11 years his senior, for two years, during which time their daughter Sarah was born. His much-publicized relationship with Julia Roberts (see page 49) ended three days before their scheduled wedding day.

➤ Regular hangout: College Grill in L.A.
➤ Getaway spot: a 300-acre ranch in Whitefish, Montana
➤ What he does to relax: plays pool
➤ Fave music: Pink Floyd
➤ Transportation: dark blue 1967 Chevy Malibu convertible

Notable Quote

"In my work I have a lot of experience, but I think I probably have a lot of shortcomings in other areas."

So You Want to Know —

What that ring is Kiefer wears? It's a gold signet ring that's a variation on his family crest. The Latin word for "endure" is inscribed on the inside.

Cool Credits

➤ **Film:** *The Bay Boy* (a Canadian feature in which he debuted at 16); *At Close Range; Stand By Me; The Lost Boys; The Killing Time; Promised Land; Bright Lights, Big City; 1969; Young Guns; Young Guns II; Flashback; Renegades; Chicago Joe and the Showgirl; Flatliners; Article 99; A Few Good Men*

· ·

Kiefer Sutherland
c/o CAA
9830 Wilshire Blvd.
Beverly Hills, CA 90212

· ·

Patrick Swayze

Patrick Swayze is a talented dancer as well as actor, and was taking dance lessons before he turned six. Growing up in Texas, he got a lot of razzing about it, since those Texas dudes generally equated dancing with the word "sissy." Now that he's made it big in movies, though, Patrick doesn't have to work so hard to defend his right to be himself.

So You Want to Know —

More about Patrick's dancing career? He performed as an ice skater before heading to New York, where he danced with several dance troupes. He had to quit when his knees began causing him pain—he'd previously had three operations for football injuries and at one time almost had his leg amputated!

Super Stats

➤ Nickname: Buddy
➤ Birth date: August 18, 1952
➤ Born and raised in: Houston, Texas
➤ Family: has been happily married to dancer/actress Lisa Niemi since 1976
➤ Rock idol: Bruce Springsteen
➤ Secret fantasy: to be a rock star
➤ Songwriting credit: wrote the song "She's Like the Wind" for *Dirty Dancing*

Cool Credits

➤ **Film highlights:** *Skatetown, USA; The Outsiders; Red Dawn; Youngblood; Dirty Dancing; Steel Dawn; Next of Kin; Road House; Ghost; Point Break; City of Joy*

Notable Quote

"Passion and power are what I believe in. I put passion and power into everything I do."

Patrick Swayze
c/o Lemond Zetter
8370 Wilshire Blvd.
Beverly Hills, CA 90211

Christy Turlington

■ ■ ■ ■ ■ ■ ■ ■ ■   ■ ■

*C*hristy hadn't even dreamed of modeling when somebody snapped her picture while she was competing in a horse show. That photo ended up at a modeling agency, and before she knew it, she was getting booked. In her first year after joining Ford Models, Inc., she had so much work she hired a tutor to help her finish high school. Now Christy is one of the top stars in her profession!

So You Want to Know —

What other models say about her? "I think she's the most beautiful girl I've ever seen," says best friend Linda Evangelista, "and she has the biggest heart."

Notable Quote

"Most people have the idea that models aren't very smart, but to get to the top in any profession you have to be smart."

Super Stats

➤ Birth date: January 2, 1969
➤ Born and raised in: the East Bay area of San Francisco, and Miami, Florida
➤ Height: 5'10"
➤ Romantic connections: boyfriend is actor and screenwriter Roger Wilson (his initials are tattooed on her ankle!)
➤ Loves: dancing at the Roxy
➤ Obsessions: using the gym equipment in her apartment
➤ Collects: pottery from the twenties and thirties
➤ Fave dinner: Kentucky Fried Chicken, mashed potatoes, and beer
➤ Modeling pluses: a beautifully symmetrical face and a perfect nose
➤ Other talents: miming—she's been called "Rubberface"
➤ Post-modeling goals: to be a writer

• •

Christy Turlington
c/o Ford Models, Inc.
344 E. 59th St.
New York, NY 10022

• •

Kristi Yamaguchi

Fourth-generation American Kristi Yamaguchi was trying her luck on ice at the age of six. Even back then she saw herself as a star. But she hasn't become America's favorite figure skater simply by dreaming! She had a major dose of determination, too, not to mention a mom who was equally dedicated. Carole Yamaguchi would wake up every morning at 3:45 A.M. in order to drive her daughter to the rink by 5 A.M. so that she would have fresh ice to practice on. That devotion—of both mother and daughter— has paid off. Kristi was competing by the age of eight, and throughout high school, she spent five hours each morning on the ice before going to school. She performed as a pairs skater for years, was twice a national champion, and these days is the coolest thing on ice skates!

Career Coups

➤ 1986 U.S. Junior Champion in pairs skating
➤ 1988 U.S. Junior Champion in pairs skating
➤ 1988 World Junior Champion in both pairs and singles skating events
➤ at the 1989 World Championships, became the first U.S. citizen to qualify in two events
➤ 1991 World Champion in singles
➤ in 1992, won both the U.S. and the World Championships in singles and won the Olympic Gold Medal in singles
➤ endorses Kellogg's Special K breakfast cereal

Notable Quote

"Having to get up so early and work so hard has been an equal trade-off because of what I've gotten back through skating."

So You Want to Know —

About the first obstacle Kristi ever overcame? Though you would never suspect it today when you watch Kristi's fancy footwork, she was born with club feet. Fortunately, her parents put her into a pair of special shoes, and the problem was quickly corrected.

Super Stats

➤ Birth date: July 12, 1971
➤ Birthplace: Hayward, California
➤ Hometown: Fremont, California
➤ Hair/eye color: Black/brown
➤ Height: 5'
➤ Family: father, Jim, is a dentist and mother, Carole, is a medical secretary; older sister, Lori, and brother, Brett
➤ Education: Missies San Jose High School
➤ Trains in: Edmonton, Alberta (Canada)
➤ Coach: Christy Ness

• •

Kristi Yamaguchi
c/o U.S. Figure Skating Association
20 First St.
Colorado Springs, CO 80906

• •

Photo Credits: